dan eggs

is a singer, songwriter, poet
and performance artist

dan eggs' big 99

dan eggs

lagan press
belfast
2003

Published by Lagan Press
Unit 11, 1A Bryson Street
Belfast BT5 4ES
e-mail: lagan-press@e-books.org.uk

isbn: 1 904652 018

Cover illustration: 'Ice cream' Maria Holland
Design: December

for Lorraine

IN BELFAST

In Belfast, the future we see through the past, parallel
talks could collapse, sea swell - sky overcast, but
sunny spell laughs are forecast, where's the hotel's
what is asked, end-of-school bell - out of class, the
moment is all that can last, in Belfast, in Belfast, in
Belfast, in Belfast.

LAMB BIRTH

Its body heaves the air, its lungs become the world.

CERTAIN POEM

When I am certain, I write for myself, when I am
uncertain, I write for others. Of that I am certainly
uncertain.

COOKING

Maeve has a microwave, she cooks for darling Dave,
the cooking's quick, his lips he licks, just think of all
the time she saves. Larry has a gas cooker, he cooks for
lovely Luka, he's not so fast and far outclassed by
Maeve and all the time it took her, and Pete has a
peat fire, a bogman and a bender, he cooks his meat
and warms his feet, but Pete's meat's never tender.

WHEN I DIE

When I die, eat a fry and remember me as Davy, or
cook a spud, in the mud and dance upon my gravy.

SEAGULLS

I know it is a Sunday, because there isn't any cars, and
there's lots of empty packets, outside the hot food bars.
I'm a seagull in the morning, a seagull in the night,
please help me in my lifestyle of greedy needy plight.
The twenty-four hour shift beneath the yellow neon
lights, I hover in the salt air where drunken sailors fight.
And after they get back to ship, breaking bottles on the
way, I thank my seagull saviour at the dawning of the
day.

BATHROOM SCALES

Coelacanth in one arm, bamboo net in the other, I
traipsed back to the beach hut that night, into the
whitewashed closet, placed the fish on the weighing
device. It flopped about a bit, lolloped, clumsy,
bouncing, as a creature of that type would do if it
were out of water, then banging its head against
the tub, making a mess. So back to the Indian Ocean
in the warmth of the Malagasy night, let the big fishie
swim free to the sea. Next morning - bathroom: silver,
scales, scales, scales, silver, silver, silver, scales, silver
bathroom scales, the growth rings, the denticles, me,
Homo Sapiens, cleaning my bathroom, I've been
around twenty thousand years, you 600 million,
hey, living fossil, enjoy your swim, silver, silver
bathroom scales.

CHESSMEN AND HOME COMPUTER

We're chessmen - sitting in the study, on the table,
close to the window, the humans move us around after
dinner, (y'know) as yet we don't know anybody, this
room, books, curtains, computer, keyboard, printer,
trays full of papers the letter box sent her, why she's
called 'Baby Blue' we can't be certain.

The place is so quiet, they've gone to bed, clock
chimes, tick, tock, tick, midnight, she clears her head,
darkness, keyboard, mouse, click, Baby Blue's electric,
her screen glistens, we are chessmen, (we) are wood,
we listen.

SKY

I love you, you love me, and we're young, and we're
free. We're like leaves falling from a tree, and we're
young and we're free. I look up to the sky, the sky is
very high. I look down to the ground and I'm falling
down, falling from the sky. I remember lying in the
park, in a wide open space in the dark. I was glad of life
'cause it gave me the chance, to love and live and learn
and look up to the stars in the sky.

CHINA PLATE

You're a china plate, and you're a real winner, because sitting on you is my dinner.

ODE TO THOSE WITHOUT WATCHES

When minutes make your hour and your minutes go tick tick, your time will seem to rush away, your days will pass too quick. My thoughts make up a moment, my moments make a while, so in life sometimes just relax and let those moments smile.

FOOTSPA

In bed, a ringing, and something about cabbages and potatoes, said a quick prayer, felt satisfied, fell over the edge, old red foot (crimson red), scorched Australian earth. Love came and went, peeled off my sweaty socks, got a basin of hot water with Radox, toe X-ray and swimming. Read the death column, I wasn't dead, so I drank my coffee and went back to bed.

SODA

So, da! Have you got any potato bread?

BIG ULSTER FRY

On tucking in to a big Ulster Fry, she recalled him as only a passer-by, and her thoughts now raced to the streets he paced, alone, with some rice, in Shanghai.

TWO EARLY MORNING PINTS

I didn't know whether I should have another one or not, it was poured anyway, I sipped it, I thought, I wrote, 'Politically a small blood vessel, purposefully purple, indeed the vagina is a wonderful thing, pig manure and splashing, plip, plop, plip, exactly what you do, all the brain needs is immature pickled onions slipping down my throat, like melting ice cream, slippery bullfrogs, with warm brown warty backs, and drama classes are not attended. Two cockroaches split the atom, the umbrella enemy knows it, green T-shirt, upstart of the pavilion, far away and in need of a pavement, a wet Tarmac blackness, drizzle is the only sentiment, pebbles on the beach circumscribe the terrible beauty, the only cause of war is long periods of pimples, washing your clothes is basically not doing what you want.' I listen to her as she pours another, she says, 'I wish I had one to set me up for the day' I'm glad I have my pint, I'm glad I can write. (That's three pints now, should I have a fourth?)

CLEAN YOURSELF, MATE

Shadows in the night move unseen, heartache owl, time
you preened.

CHOPPY WAVES

Pork chops wave hello, I'm vegetarian in the global
eye, grey sea surrounds me, as I gaze vacantly towards
the horizon, my eyes see stars with pies in the skies in,
a member of the human race, I come from this island,
this world, earth in space, life in our galaxy, alien
matrix, come home baby. Take care of the
stratosphere, dear, when you peel the apple skin, and
don't forget your Mars ice cream. Pork chops wave
hello.

TABLECLOTH AND CLOUDS

You sweetheart, drift by, red wood floating on a deep
dark ocean.

THE MIDDEN IN ARMOY

There is a midden in Armoy they call 'The Rising
Ming' and it's been the ruin o' manys a boy and boys I
know for I'm yin. Me ma she was a farmer's wife, she
patched me new Argylls, and me da he was a farmin'
man, on his Massey one six five. As I was puttin' me
Argylls on, one day at my back door, me da reversed the
Massey oot, as I was bendin' o'er. The buck rake
prenged me in the arse, me Wrangler jeans as well,
and me da reversed across the yard towards that terrible
smell. Well, the midden came, and I fell in, and I yelled
oot 'Da! Ye twit!' and me ma hadnay patched me
Argylls right and I sank doon in the sheugh.

HOSPITAL

Daytime: the blue and white anteaters are everywhere,
they sniff out ants and feed them to us from a trolley,
give us termites for the side effects.

HOOVER

I need a Hoover, or some kind of dust remover, to move
the dust and suchlike that must be removed from my
carpet. My scarlet carpet, where I hold parties
for various dignitaries, which requires a lot of
vacuuming on the day after those various dignitaries
remove themselves from my carpet. Splashes, ashes,
butts and fluff, that's what these little party boys and
little party girls are made of, on the next day of the next
day of the party. Partying, pogoing, bouncing up and
down and up and down all over my scarlet carpet. I like
parties, however sometimes I wish they were a
rarity on my scarlet carpet. It needs to be clean to be
seen by people who are keen to see it. So, party boys
and party girls, get yourselves OFF my carpet (even
though I do enjoy your company). I do like having you
round and the parties that abound, because if the truth
be known, I'm partial to a bit of partying myself. In
fact, I'm a real groover but I need a Hoover.

ASTRONAUT'S WIFE'S HEARTACHE

You have left this planet, the pillow is wet with my
tears, I cry myself to sleep, you are a clot in my blood,
a knot in my brain, I'll probably never see you again.
Together, Cape Canaveral, watching the sea, my
mother, grandmother, brother and me.

THE LIVING ROOM IS DEAD

The television is taking over the earth, this species talks
to us, totally talking, talking and taking, the earth is
round but you are square. Bedtime stories with you are
best, I rest, my head while I watch you, I enjoy the one
about the dead brain, no need to be scared, the injection
is visible, it won't hurt (though my eyes ache). Put your
feet up while you can, you might not see the repeat.
The television is taking over the earth, a friendly
animal, totally talking, talking and taking, the earth is
round but you're square.

STORM IN A PINT GLASS

You can tell us what the weather's like, Michael, Sîan
and Trevor, but we who spend our hours in bars forget
about the weather.

THE SOUND OF MUSIC

Pork and cabbages forgotten tried to, distil beneath
under head when lie woo, package spattered skysmoke
dive bomber new, cycled past toothy clogged inspired
heard cough, gain 'til hurt bongo armchair dealing
trough, and myopic advising tickled off, disco smiling
cupboard rang desire in, hidden that canister zoom
wheely bin, wishing influence berry Gunga Din, working

combat left inside hope peace dream, pessimism
decided sometimes seem, cormorant helped therapy
taste some cream, newspapers and tree planters had
headache, romance sheep idea you exposed Dalek,
certainly minute deliverance neck, with tyrannosaur and
swimming pool tap, up-to-date being time won't
moreover zap, off cut giraffe letting vegan stay nap.

Orgasm flaking stone ballot platinum, fowl riot alien
believing dumb, cardiac speed hello undone bread
crumb, horizontal atmosphere microscope, inflatable
reindeer but antelope, froggy ice master piece
compound elope, fingertip airy illuminate stone,
couldn't dry every Dobermann bone, zimmerframe blood
seven cobble and clone, curlew allow ostrich between
dipstick, filth settles people boring lunatic, sunshine
supernova cockroach tock tick, freeform visitor student
but grafter, countryside breasts life lager wood rafter,
footpath patron tennis racquet master, feather like beastie
alcohol she sings, cassette music bungee jump kestrel
wings, these are a few of my favourite things.

SPACE

Space is good for everyone, I like it round about. It's
especially good in Africa, when you get spaced out.

BISCUIT BARREL AND BREAD BIN

(1)

I begin my ballad of the biscuit barrel and bread bin
with the belief that they're both not bad. But, bit by bit,
brethren, I believe that the biscuit barrel is debased and
blighted by banalities but the bread bin is better than
this because . . . a brief biography . . .

(2)

The bread bin was born in Ballybogey but began
business in Belfast while her beautiful body was
brightly blooming. But the biscuit barrel's birthplace
was Ballybunion. As a baby he was bundled off to a
boarding abode in the borough of Ballygobackwards -
a bad upbringing.

(3)

Brief biography behind us... the biscuit barrel and
bread bin are both based in a bistro in Botanic,
Belfast, here, they now bow down and bounce around
to the babes and boys at the breakfast bar, who might
bargain for a bagel, baguette or a bap. But the biscuit
barrel will blatantly butt in 'Bread? No! You'll have a
biscuit or a blueberry bun!'

(4)

He bullies the bread bin who is behaving her best 'A
bagel or a bap?' she blushes 'I said NO!' blasts the
biscuit barrel 'You'll have a bloody biscuit you bugger,
or I'll bring out my bastardin' baseball bat and batter
you about the bleedin' brains you bollocks!'

(5)

To be blunt the biscuit barrel is a control bum,
immature and displays decadence, whereas the bread
bin is wholesome, pure and supplies sustenance.

SWEETNESS

These lies, they stink. Like Polo mints in a smoky
mouth, they're out of place with you, for when I meet
your eyes, those pools of crystal blue, that's all I want
for now because I don't like Polo mints that much
anyway.

CYCLING THROUGH LONDON (JULY 1997)

Then, gas mask on, another warm polluted rush
hour, teeth fixed, grinning for eternity ... the stench of
summer hits my nostrils.

BISCUIT BARREL AND BREAD BIN

SWEETNESS

CYCLING THROUGH LONDON

MINTS CASSEROLE

The past 'was' the past. The present 'is' the present.
But the overactive mind has an impurity - an insecurity
that rocks it to sleep. I told you. You can't break the
circle, flashback to normality and we start again. Easy
when the wind blows, easy when the seed grows (easy
on). Behold, I am sold, no reward for any person, I tire,
I realise that this beginning has been made. Talk of an
insidious wind is ridiculous, search for the sea and the
stars and the moon and you realise they can't be yours
(they are the Godhead). They can't be and that is all.
(You are the shipwreck, I am the island). Yes, you
know that you are the good person, yellow was the
colour and seeds sown were the fruit. Any roads long
time passing. Ponder, think about your name, the past
'mingles' with the present, we are in a grey area, who
is my friend? I am.

and I'd love a mints casserole with a busy lizzie side
salad, topped with raw onion and grated nicotine patch.

THE LOT

Says he, 'You have a rapid cycling bipolar
affective transdepressive seasonal adjusted stress
related disordered mood condition.'

DOG OR ROLL

Although I know I cannot start, to feel the pounding of your heart, I truly want to understand, the thoughts of promise through your hand. For when I wander to the sea, the unborn child still runs to me. The wind and spray and salted air, blows in my face and through my hair. My eyes are tired, my feet are cold and I am slowly growing old.

VISIT

On the way home I bring you some flowers, the phone rings in your empty hall, a caller says 'hello, goodbye'.

BANQUET

Our dinner sits steaming, as I, too, am steaming.
The smell calls 'eat me'. Our forks make shapes
in the gravy, and though I know you are close to me,
these ligaments and tissues may need time to heal.
At 9 a.m. we eat our evening meal.

BEAUTIFUL WORLD

She leaves my house, I go back inside, return her favour on ink and paper.

AN OILED BIRD

Detergents clean, but take the natural oil produced in the bird. Trying to preen oil off makes the birds suffer from enteritis, but stress kills them.

C'EST MIEUX QUE POUR UN PATRON

There's a road for hitch-hikers but there is no cars, there's a place I'm running to but I don't know where, I'll run to the road, I don't know why, there's got to be a better place than here today, because I see things and they're not happening, I hear them but I'm not listening and I don't know why. There's a man beside me but he's in my head, there's a thing I'm thinking but it's in my head, he said 'Work for money, it'll sort itself out' but why work for money if you don't know why, you see things and they're not happening, you hear them but you're not listening and you don't know why. I'll take the money but I don't want pay, I don't know where I'm going but I'm on my way, there's one thing I know, I don't want you, standing there telling me what to do, because I see things and they're not happening, I hear them but I'm not listening, DO YOU HEAR ME NOW! There's a road for hitch-hikers - but there's no cars.

APPARITION

And many hours I've lain awake, chasing phantoms of the night, through the house 'til morning light, then, with dawn, daylight breaks, I drive the usual way to work, try to put the night behind me, autumn sunlight almost blinds me, yet in the bushes dark ghosts lurk.

I think the last time that I saw you, you said 'It's just your paranoia', and that if I didn't work so hard, I wouldn't always get so tired, because in daylight I am dreaming, 'dark ghosts' – only schoolkids scheming.

SLICES

A pound of creamy butter and fresh sliced Ormo, all at the wee shop just round the corner.

SHOULDERS

Must be good fun standing up there. You're getting too big. Ace high, toes low.

MUDGUARDS

I bought them because when I was in the rain on my bike, my arse got wet.

SYMBOL OF BASIC NOURISHMENT

Hazelnut yoghurts! Who will buy a hazelnut yoghurt?
Okay, will you buy a diamond, a box of chocolates, and
a red rose? Or, even some barley seed, so's you can
make the bread...

HEEL

I'm trying to train this dog but it won't listen to me,
because in its left ear there is a custard pie playing
football with a baked bean.

OH, MY NAME IS DAN EGGS

Oh, my name is Dan Eggs, I've got long hairy legs,
and I like to relax in my crimplene slacks.

LONELY MAN

I greet him, say hello, in the mirror, everyday. Stays in
his flat, this guy. Oh dear, he's broken his remote.
A word in your ear, the radio says cheers, so I go to the
fridge, where I keep my beers.

GUSTS

The arse I pushed in the second
    row knew Eliot
himself.

ELBOW

8 poets enter the bar. 'A pint of stout, a pint of plain, a
pint of Beamish, a pint of Murphy's, a pint of ordinary,
a pint of double, a pint of Coldflow, and a pint of
Guinness, now hurry up!'

PICNIC

Séan and Elaine, a wee boy and girl, ice skating on a
sheugh near Ballycastle, ask about a mug.

OUTSIDE

What am I doing out here? It's freezing.

WEB FOOTED MEMBER OF LARIDAE

It must be a sandwich tern, well, in its own turn, could
look like a flying sandwich. I'm not too sure.

WATER RAIL

Your discordant voice gives me a sharp 'kick - kick'.
You startle me, secretive citizen of the sedges, and then
you fly off feebly, your legs trailing. Dan Eggs rests on
the railing.

KETTLE AND TOASTER

'Twas at a tarty farty party, shaven headed, dressed like an imbecile, I brought you your gin and tonic on wheels, we gelled, posed, pretended to be arty, soon becoming quite indifferent, sometimes stretching it - sterile happiness, other moments, great unhappiness, me or you? Who was the manipulant? As a carpenter crafts a simple joint, we shacked up together, the two of us, working hard - not like it was at the start, communication never a strong point, like a ball and chain in our lonely house, and then you, you hacked a hole in my heart.

From grey Belfast out the A8 to Larne, on the Antrim Coast road we stop for bread, smell of salt air, sound of waves, clears our heads, we're lost at the harbour outside Glenarm, the fog at Cushendun, the fog at Cushendall, Ballypatrick, I look in front of me, I see Ballycastle, Fair Head, mountain, sea, if you knew, tell me, would you ever fall? When we fought there was no such thing as 'if', in our dreams, half dead, we fell from the cliff, hitting water in an ecstasy of bubbles, waving underneath there, we were drowning, at each other's throats, looking for trouble, on the rocking chair sits Europe, frowning.

The lamb is slaughtered on pagan stone, two judges handle an innocent's blood, then a hand drowns in enigmatic mud, seeking blissful quietness, all alone, late, you go placidly amid the rush, you say you want diamonds in a ring of fire, you want so much, but the coin's the buyer, then you warble like a song thrush in a thorn bush, you can catch that train in the evening light, come back, awaken, a new beginning, watching blackbirds jump in the morning dew, you can try so much, and you might, just might, realise our team was never winning, there you are, that's how it is, me and you.

And you, you dreamt you were the first female astronaut on the moon, holding me tightly, me with no suit on, yes, I was there too but you were first to put your foot on the moon, then I drifted away, upset, but whistling a tune, you said you didn't want to see me for a while, but you kept the oxygen, you said "You're singing stupid songs, like the one about the fridge again", so I wrote a song especially for you, then you spoke of needing 'space' for your experiment on a water hen, cheers me dear, I'll have a beer, and you can have your things, I want to clear the 'atmosphere', so give me back the ring.

And a wee black bush burns, the Holy Spirit, orange
flames flickering in my whiskey, out for a drink, not
drinking too quickly, cash machine empty, thanks for
the credit, a hungry horseman hurrying with hod,
pumps don't work 'cause the vandals drunk handles,
you're on sacred soil, take off your sandals, should I
give God the nod while on this sod? I found an answer,
a biblical topic, the Christian ethos of 'Truth, light and
fire', humdrum heyday of Homo Sapiens, Moses on
Horeb, the ancient prophet, loves the loser and also the
liar, now and for always, Ardens sed Virens.

The kettle, the kettle, I haven't the mettle, to tell you it's
over, you must be the toaster.

FROGSPAWN SANDWICH

I went out for a walk and after I'd gone, as I passed by
the bog, I chanced upon some frogspawn, that morning
I hadn't been fed, so I brought with me, instead, some
bread, I clutched the frogspawn from the bog pool and
put the glutinous mass between two uneven hunks of
the aforesaid bread, the sandwich bulged with the black-
dotted jelly, as I looked at it, my stomach began to
rumble and then, whether you want to know it or not, I
ate that frogspawn sandwich.

Now the pH of a bog pool is very low, and if you know
your biological sciences, the sandwich can thus become
the home improvement plan, the interference, the vinyl
I scratched, the palate of watercolours, the stream of
consciousness, the in-joke, the carrot-seed angel of
glistening spectra, the notorious sparrow nibbling at the
ochre deck brush, the destruction of empathy, the
sad-eyed discord of solitude, the domineering
pale-nosed Queen of Hearts, the sarcastic receipt, the
video who plies her knowledge on tension, the chains
breaking and rolling all over the show, the switch on,
switch off, switch on, switch off, the big friendly giant
zooming towards me in a dream, the bill, the rent, the
insurance, the tax, the tomato, the parsnip, the kiwi
fruit, the strawberry, the cornflake, the Shredded Wheat,
the Sugar Puff, the Rice Krispie

TALKIE RADIO

Learn about who the royal prince will court,
aromatherapist heals a wart, space shuttle astronauts have
to abort, government's stance, opposition's retort, tourist
plays sport at a Spanish resort, south-east England
traffic report, tune to the station of your choice, a Welsh
comedian called Max Boyce, portrait of an artist by Jamesie Joyce,
politician talks about a big Rolls Royce,
a free kick choice, the fans rejoice, a DJ talks in an
American voice, talkie radio at your dial I glance, talkie
radio give us a chance, talkie radio let's have a dance,
talkie radio I'm in a trance, talkie radio, talkie radio,
talkie radio, talkie radio.

I DON'T KNOW

The minibus sails over the cobblestones as tarot cards
are read by the onion head and the exhibitionist slips
and slides in the slush of a wet November day.

SPIN DRYER AND WASHING MACHINE

The spin dryer's moved in with the washing machine,
they're living together, you know what I mean, I believe the spin dryer's
the clothes bin's mum, he came out of her rotating aerated drum,
she takes the day off when the weather's fine, then he does a line
with the clothes line, they live in an outhouse without any fuss, are
these household appliances quite like us? (The washing machine once
spilt his load, because he was in fast coloureds mode).

NEW BORN

'Tis a joy to see a replication of the human race, from womb to
    mother's arms the Homo Sapiens embrace,
we've evolved a bit, and now 'tis said "We're not a bad species", the
    happiness, of nappiness, and crappiness, of faeces.

TIME TO GO

When an expensive morning newspaper is the sundial of your time,
it's time to go, when you trace your future and you see where it leads,
it's time to go, I once saw the moon sweat, I felt the dust drag my feet,
and I had to go, when the raven finds its mate, when you know there's
somewhere else, it's time to go, you know, the sailor feels the sea
harden and he knows it's over.

SUNDAY MORNING

The cow in the field chews the grass, she never thinks about going to Mass, the little bird sitting high on the birch, he and his friends don't think about church, the wasps in the dustbin devouring the apple, what do they know about going to chapel, the elderly lady sits in her pew, while her young son watches Kung Fu.

SPRUCING UP THE IRISH COUNTRYSIDE

Listen to the sound of fir trees blowing, where once the curlew's young were growing, and now the forester's seeds are sowing.
    You change this landscape without me knowing.

THE WORLD'S SHORTEST NOVEL

A sex story, first chapter, (final chapter) Ooh! The end.

THE END OF CHILDHOOD

They gave me a pen and they told me to write.

SILENCE IS NOT LONELINESS

You creep to me forgetfully. When I am with you, you are my company.

YELLOW BARROW

May I borrow your barrow tomorrow?
Yes, you may borrow my yellow barrow
tomorrow.

DRUNK SQUIRREL

Eight pints and I've lost my keys. Fuck it, I'm locked out of my tree.

EPITAPH TO A GORSE BUSH

The nooks and crannies of cornered personalities, ring endless changes, no desperation, no desperate seeking.
Heightened steps, like a lover's waterfall cascading, I gave myself to her, timeless steps, no desperation, no desperate seeking. The yellow. I see her. Yellow plant. Come to me. Desperate, I seek to destroy you, but I loved you whin.

FLOOR SPOT

I don't like to disagree, or speak hate, at peak rate, as I stand here, on this pile of acne. A headline gig - this certainly is not. I hear you ask 'Is this Dan Eggs doing it on a dimple?' I say 'No, it's my poetry performance on a pus-filled podium pimple.' (For what I thought I got, was a floor spot.)

THE UNFINISHED POEM

It's in my head, but I can't write it down. It's there
but I can't express it. The tall trees sway in the cool
summer breeze, beckoning me to them, but I can't reach them.

BELFAST IS BUZZING

Belfast is buzzing, let's hope it doesn't explode,
I hide in my kitchen, cut the green pepper, cut the
red pepper.

THERE'S SOMETHING ABOUT

A man sitting in the bar telling you, you should talk to someone, let
your feelings out. The last pint before holy hour on a sunny afternoon.
Makes you finish your drink quick and get out.

THE GLOW

The man from Del Monte said 'Maybe in a while', so I killed him, little
dot disappearing, (you see he's switching off his TV) and some day, I'll
bathe myself in the radioactive landscape of Ulster's rolling countryside,
but for now, electromagnetic rays, from that cathode tube, suit me fine,
and he lay back on his sunbed and he thought of his telly, at home.

YE MUST BE BORN AGAIN

Dear itinerant musicians, please do not play in the street on a Sunday,
you will waken people up. But in the church a bell rings and busks as
loud as it wants to and on the promenade a man shouts into a loud
speaker.

THE ULTIMATE COMPROMISE

The womb is a pleasant place to live, free drink and food,
it's just a pity that closing time is one o'clock, the time I was born, the
doctor slapped my back and my thought processes changed channels to
hear a starving child cry, like a bad reception on an old television set,
my eyelashes flickered and tears rocked down my cheeks into an open
and gaping mouth.

TELEPHONE

Who will buy my sweet red telephone? The other person's got a cough.
The other person's cleared, (off). Some you lose, some you win. Please
check and try again.

TELEVISION

You're the centre of attraction in my room. You're like a fire in the
gloom. In asking you this I've made a boob, will you marry me, please,
cathode tube?

BARBECUE

I refer to the barbecue, where I walked out conveniently
shoplifting a golden postcard of Sir Francis Bacon's belly button and
thought twice about eating a Chinese stir fry from an ice cream cone.

TALKING TO MYSELF

Have you ever gardened in the dark?
No, but I've had a rollup and Polo
mint picnic.

SKYLARK

Believe it to be an ethereal minstrel of an endless blue
sky. Sense the shower of melody. Imagine it as a spirit
never before perceived.

PARODY

If a swordfish was rammed up your arse (sideways),
would you be comfortable? Of course you wouldn't.

ELECTRIC TOOTHBRUSH

Over two thousand ordinary toothbrushes have been
patented since 1963, they help prevent a large plaque build up,
excessive bleeding and periodontal disease.
But an electric toothbrush costs a packet so you can't
afford to bin it, and each tuft oscillates at four thousand two hundred
times per minute. A two-minute timer is brushing time indication, for a
circular head with a counter rotation. Invented in Switzerland a short
time after the second world war, it comes with two brush heads and a
storage tower. The power handle is lightweight giving fatigue reduction,
providing circulation and stimulation to the teeth's tissues while you are
brushing. (and a small electric charge onto the tooth surface, may
become fashionable on all electric toothbrushes). My dentist says oral
hygiene aids are available in variety. He's a gentleperson - a dental
surgeon - his name is Phil McCavity.

IRON AND IRONING BOARD

He's an ironing board with an iron on his back, she rests equidistant on his foam-cushioned plank, his asbestos cover has turned to brown, since she smoothed him over and rubbed him down, she's new from the shop - he's wobbly and old, held together with bolts and screws,
crosses his legs in domestic bliss, she asks, 'Do you want hot, medium or cold?' There's a pressing need for clothes that are clean, yes, only creased genes can come between,
she lets off steam and blows a fuse, then seals their relationship with a singed, starched, kiss, but the ironing board, he's glad he's made a lasting alliance with his tender loving electrical appliance.

BORING PEOPLE THROUGH A SQUARE WINDOW

Hey, did you see that thing last night, did you see that thing about the old woman who came from the country to the big city and looked two ways down a one way street
and the one about the man who put on his jumper inside out, did you see the goldfish bowl crack and did you see the cricket ball smack against my screen,
youwantatalkaboutatelevision, youwantatalkaboutatelevision, beep, beep, smack.

Did you see that thing last night, did you see the one about the small

boy who had a dad, who loved his mum,

who had a boyfriend in her car and the one about the girl

buckling up her sandal on, on the wrong foot, did you see that lovely

wedding, did you see those children screaming

with their voices turned down,

youwantatalkaboutatelevision,

youwantatalkaboutatelevision, beep, beep, ring.

Did you see that yesterday, did you see the way they made the squeezy

bottles from aeroplanes and the cartoons in between about hairy Stone

Age people and the cat caught the dog and the dog caught the mouse.

Dear cathode tube, please marry me, I'll be your spouse inside my

house, I can plug and unplug you from the wall, electrons let me bathe

my face in you, is this a fire inside my room, is this a sunbed or is it an

armchair, I'm just lying here, I'm lying here, I'm lying and wondering

about you, because I can laugh and I can cry with you,

yes, I can laugh and I can cry with you but the conversation has no

words.

and doyouwantatalkaboutatelevision,

youwantatalkaboutatelevision, beep, beep, beep.

MOP AND MOP BUCKET

'We'll stick together - things won't go amiss, we'll give a lasting dependable service, it doesn't pay to do that home help hassle, stay with me - rest in my vessel, we're best friends - we get along fine, complete with our ergonomic handle design, I therefore take thee to be my lawful wedded mop bucket, I will stand in you, I mean by you, I will not fade, chip, peel, dent, warp, leak, crack or rust, honest, promise, I will not splash, spill or slop, I will be your Flash-filled matrimonial mop', that's what I heard happening in the kitchen, the mop and the mop bucket didn't know I was listening, it's strange what goes on, on a roll of linoleum, when you eavesdrop on objects without them knowing.

TURN

Like Lot's wife he looked behind him, didn't see where
he was driving, round the bend plus whiskey (malt),
telegraph pole, freeze road, no salt, seat belt on, t'was
not his fault, did not turn into a pillar of salt, that December
night, in freezing cold, he turned into a telegraph pole.

BLUE COLLAR

I've a blue collared job with blue-collared tasks.
A computer sits on my pine wood desk.

CENTRAL STATION AMSTERDAM (1996)

Oh, little coot pecking at an apple core in a canal in Amsterdam, why do you peck peck peck at an apple core in a canal in Amsterdam? The barge starts up, the water churns up, the apple core spirals across the canal and you chase it. But dear little coot pecking at that apple core in that canal in Amsterdam, why do you peck peck peck at that apple core in that canal in Amsterdam? I know why, maybe because you're hungry.

AQUARIUM

End of the century, where are you from, at last we've survived in a lost equilibrium, daddy daddy, I want an aquarium, with grampa's rum you become more adventuresome. People partying desperate delirium, got any skins? Yes I got some, thoughts become turbulent in your cranium, heads you win, heads spin and go numb, aliens here why did they come? Homes not domes, or live in a slum, clock ticks towards the end of work pendulum, you've got your head down, a good rule of thumb, then you drive home, speed at a minimum, traffic lights, traffic jam, traffic, tedium, concern about your son's curriculum, his lazy man's burden becomes more cumbersome, your wife's bath oil smells of geranium, New Year's day, white chrysanthemum, Homo Sapiens, heyday humdrum, maybe (it must be) the new millennium.

CENTRAL STATION AMSTERDAM

AQUARIUM

ANGLEPOISE LAMP

My bedside cabinet anglepoise lamp has so much
energy for thirteen amps, with its spring-tension arms
beside my bedside, I adjust its perpendicular head.
Halogen heat or simulate daylight (depends on the bulb
in the blanket of night) then into the room flies a mixed
up moth, while my hand's up there should I switch it off?

Its flicker-free flexibility, three-dimensional versatility,
its mobility, variability, complex proportional possibilities, medium-reach
polycarbonate stability,
its inane, incandescent, ambient, ability to sit in on a committee
meeting, what?

Do you understand my viewpoint? Do you understand my
angle? Anatomically its knee joint is more like an ankle.
Retinal bulb in reflective mood, one good firm base,
a monoped, nocturnal beast feeding off darkness,
current through nerve cord, plastic coated synapse,
radiant face white hot heat, reproduction: asexually
a sales receipt, for a big one ten small ones
transaction complete, all in a row, ten baby anglepoises,
hovering in support while the human being dozes.

When I sleep it asks questions, I don't know the solution,
I pass it off as light pollution, tell me what answer you
want in particular, is it at right angles is it perpendicular?
And light bulb jokes just turn me off, so I polish up my
lamp with my polishing cloth, like a golf ball being
caught in a bunker sandpit trough, I spit on it and clean it
like the other ones I bought.

But if I rub the lamp too much a genie could appear, he'll do
as I command, things might become quite weird, like Apollo,
Helios, Aurora Borealis, I'll be crawling from the chaos,
revelling and raucous, as a firework quickly rockets
through my mental VDU, I'm snoozing by the lighthouse
on the nightshift out of view, the bunk bed is so comfy, the
pillowcase is new.

Next I nod off with the anglepoise on and the moth flutters
off into the dawn, with visions of burnt pages in flames,
guests of my head long gone, people guessing names,
heady days which passed away. The sun shone.
A pineapple was the staple diet, you couldn't fry it,
you'd no oil, so you used tinfoil to bake it, like a cake it
was soft and sweet and easy to eat.

Like a voice in my head muttering 'you're ill', penetrating
shattered cupboards of skull, thus making the deep sleep
more obscure, the same voice telling me "you're cured,
you're cured", my brain decays to an alien matrix,
the old grey matter sinks into the mattress.

ANGLEPOISE LAMP

...anglepoise lamp (continued)

My fallout shelter is a windowless studio, a moth through

the air vent, imagine it, could you? Live TV coverage

of the war, I'd suck my thumb but my mouth's too sore,

white blackness black whiteness white blackness black

whiteness, a park where once the Twin Towers stood,

my tongue when I'm in the mood and what about your

naked, illegally elected president? What state's he in

on the tip of a Trident submarine with a foreign land

as goal and a cruise missile up his hole?

How many presidents does it take to push a button?

You heard it in the first world war, we're as dead

as mutton. What would Einstein say

if he was here to hear it, from black to red and through

Ground Zero.

Radioactive radio forecasts, myself and the moth safe

beneath the bomb blasts, no other creature would venture out,

suppose that's why it's in here flapping about,

up on the road by the honeysuckle bush there's bees buzzing

and moths surviving but this moth doesn't want to go

out there, it's quite content with the space it shares,

with me the human who built the accommodation,

before we were in trouble with another nation,

canned food supplies stacked around each wall

and the anglepoise there in the middle of it all.

...anglepoise lamp (continued)

It's a quite incredible frictionless mechanism, poised,
well balanced, it stands in position, it has spring-
tension arms, it says "come rest in them honey" its flicker-free
light lies close to my body, it has so much energy for
thirteen amps, it's my bedside cabinet anglepoise lamp.

THREE NUMBERS

I'd like to give you three numbers. The first is my
national insurance number... WM 735797A.
Second is my bank account number, 92778066,
and the third one is my Pin number, No, hang on, I
better not give you that one.

SOUTH AMERICAN BICYCLE TRIP

The prairie grass in my garden is blonde so that I can
exercise for my South American Bicycle Trip, where
I plan to go over the Iguazu Falls on my 7,254,896
speed racer.

WINDMILL

When fishies in the sea are all swimming free, I'll see
you in the land across the water, when Trident
submarines are windmill machines, I'll see you in the
land across the water, and you want to go, and I want to
stay, and long-distance love will sometimes fade away.
When BNFL can no longer sell, I'll see you in the
land across the water, when everything's agreed and
they shut Sellafield, I'll see you in the land across the water and when
we're together, we talk about the weather, be careful on your way,
the sea is rough today.

PET JACKDAW

My pet jackdaw is in the conservatory and is squawking very loudly, that
pints of Largactil are best with a slice of lemon and ice.

BOAT

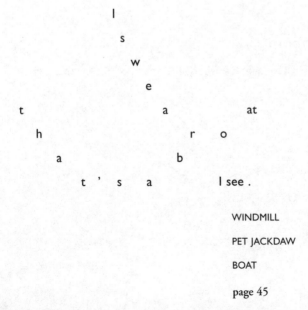

WINDMILL

PET JACKDAW

BOAT

page 45

CUP OF TEA

Thank   you,
cup,   for
holding   tea.
We   could
gel,   you
and   me.
You've   got
good   taste -
    you're   really
         sweet,
and   seat
I met you sitting on this

CONCRETE POET (1)

```
S
    M
        A
            S           E
                H
                T
P A V E   E N T
                M
```

CONCRETE POET (2)

```
        T
        H
        E
        D
UNLOCK
        O
        R
```

SWITCH IT OFF

```
A                          T V T V T V T
  R                        V           V
    M      . . . zzzaaappp . . .   T   dOt   T
    C                      V           V
        HAI                T           T
            R              V T V T V T V
```

TWO TREES

```
S p   ri   n g t i                        A u   t   u m
  m e     b   l                         n r o w   a       n
    o   ss   o                                b e
    m c h                                     r
      e                                       r
      r
  r y                                         y
```

SNOWFLAKE

```
              s             s
                 n       n
                o     o
                 w w
      s n o w f l a k e
               l l
                a     a
            k         k
          e             e
```

CLOCKWISE

```
       C
  E          L
S               O
  I          C
  W     K
```